Furniture Makeovers

in a weekend

Furniture Makeovers

in a weekend

Alice Hamilton

MEREHURST

Acknowledgements

Grateful thanks to Amanda Gibbs who put up with my frenzy, for all her support, hard work and patience. Thanks to William Douglas for his photographic skills and professionalism, and to his assistant, Nigel 'the hands'. Thanks to Fiona Tillett for her inspirational talents and her great sense of humour. Also to Gill Christie who came so speedily and conscientiously to the rescue with her computer skills.

First published 1997 by Merehurst Limited,
Ferry House, 51–57 Lacy Road, London, SW15 1PR

Copyright © 1997 Merehurst Limited

ISBN 1-85391-524-6

A catalogue record for this book is available from the British Library.

Editor: Geraldine Christy
Designer: Anthony Cohen
Photographer: William Douglas
(with the exception of photographs on pages 63, 66 [lower], 67, 68 & 69: courtesy of Graeme Ainscough)
Stylist: Fiona Tillett

Colour separation by Bright Arts, Hong Kong
Printed in Italy by New Interlitho S.p.A.

Contents

Introduction

Creating a warm and individual environment in which to live is one of man's basic instincts. Every society has produced and developed a cornucopia of styles and techniques with which to enhance the home. Starting a home or moving house is the beginning of a new and exciting venture; redecorating walls and adding fabric and colour are the fundamental aspects of making a personal mark on a place. Buying furniture or adapting what is already there is not as straightforward but can, nevertheless, be rewarding and challenging and need not cost the earth.

The availability of general decorating and home improvement materials has grown over the years. So, too, has the number of books and publications to tempt homeowners to acquire new skills, and to try out different techniques of decorating and construction for themselves. Sometimes it can seem a bit daunting that a whole workshop of equipment and materials is required before the work can be started.

The aim of this book is to show that a great deal can be achieved, giving impressive effects, using a few basic pieces of equipment and by learning just a few simple techniques and skills. These techniques are interchangeable – in other words, do not be restricted by what is shown in one project, as it could be applied just as suitably to another piece of furniture.

When searching in second-hand furniture shops or bric à brac markets for the pieces to work on, keep an open mind. The table or shelves you find may not be exactly what you hoped for, but look at the potential of what lies there, think of what could be achieved with the addition of a length of beading, a different top, a piece of cornice and so on. Do not be put off by a piece of furniture that looks like a hopeless cause. Woodworm can be treated and the holes filled; joints can be glued back together; tatty upholstery removed and replaced; layers of ugly paint stripped to reveal beautiful woods and fine surfaces; breakages can be mended; pieces added or taken away. Have courage, be bold – with patience and a little imagination a new creation will unfold.

The majority of paints used in the projects are water-based, unless otherwise stated. The main advantage of this is that they are quick-drying, allowing the work to be achieved over two days or so. Also, they do not have the toxic properties of oil-based materials. Artists' acrylic paints and dry pigments are used to tint acrylic all-in-one primer and undercoat paints. The advantages of doing this are twofold:

endless cans of paint are not required for each project and also paints can be mixed to your personal requirements, although in some cases, where a large quantity of paint is needed it may be easier to buy one off the shelf ready mixed.

When mixing a colour, if you are starting with a white or pale base, add the

pigments or colours to a small quantity of the base colour and mix thoroughly, gradually blending in more of the base to the required amount. A word of advice here – always mix up more paint then less, as it can be very time-consuming trying to match up a new batch later. It is also a good idea to make a note of the proportions and quantities of the colours used – this will save time if more is required, as well as being a useful record.

In approaching each project, assemble the tools and materials beforehand. There is nothing more frustrating than getting halfway through a task and discovering that a vital tool is required, or that there are not enough screws to fix something – especially when the shops are closed! On the subject of tools and brushes, it is always worth paying a little more

and acquiring better quality equipment. It saves money and time in the long run, as poor tools give poor results, will not last well and can be frustrating to work with. The same applies to paints – the better quality ones are made with higher grade pigments, which means they give a good depth of colour and better covering power.

With the abundance of literature available on house design and interiors, furniture and textiles, there is no shortage of inspirational material around to give ideas for these projects. Start with the idea and then work out ways of achieving the effect on the piece of furniture, using the practical step-by-step guides in the projects. Some of these are more labour intensive than others, but all are accessible. Look also, for inspiration, at the layout and style of the room in which the piece will eventually be placed.

Last, but not least, the projects in this book are meant to be fun to do and the results enjoyed, with satisfaction and pride that you have achieved so much from what may have been an unattractive and neglected piece of furniture.

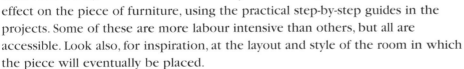

Painted curtain pole

A painted curtain pole adds a touch of luxury. Here a plain wooden pole is decorated in rich, earthy colours reminiscent of the Italian Renaissance style.

Planning your time

DAY ONE
AM: Sand surfaces and apply primer and undercoat paint

PM: Apply yellow ochre paint

DAY TWO
AM: Plait string and apply red ochre paint; apply gold size

PM: Gild sized areas; varnish

Tools and materials

DIY curtain pole kit

Medium and fine-grade sandpaper

Cord or string for pole, approximately four times the length of the pole

Thumbtacks or drawing pins

Piece of string to tie rings to when painting

Bradawl

Long screws

All-in-one primer and undercoat

Artists' acrylic colours – yellow ochre and red ochre

Gold size

Dutch metal

Paintbrushes

Artists' brush for gold size

White spirit

Soft brush for tidying excess gold leaf

Button polish and brush

Methylated spirits

'Black' wax and cloth (if required)

Varnish

I n general, designers are moving away from the idea that the supports for curtains and blinds must be concealed. These items are no longer considered as purely functional fittings that are better hidden out of sight.

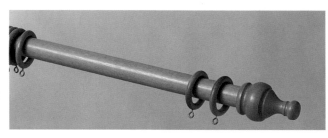

From the 18th century onwards, as plate glass became more available, architects designed broad, tall windows in buildings, bringing light and shape to the interiors of houses. The windows were then adorned with beautiful textiles, sometimes topped with splendidly decorated (and often gilded) pelmets. But there was always a place for the individually styled or decorative curtain pole, which has a wider rôle to play than merely holding up a curtain.

Nowadays a fairly wide choice of poles and finials is available. With a little imagination and colour, a plain wooden pole can become an interesting design statement. Poles can be used to drape fabric or tapestry across windows or doorways, making an attractive feature that adds to the overall decorative effect. As a finishing touch, finials can be gilded or painted to match other accessories in the room.

As well as using curtain poles to decorate windows and doors, you could put them across alcoves or above a bed to hold draped fabric, or even suspended from the ceiling as a hanging rail.

Day One

Step 1

Using medium-grade, then fine-grade, sandpaper, sand down all the pieces – the curtain pole, finials, rings and wall brackets – to provide a surface key for the paint. Apply a coat of all-in-one primer and undercoat paint to all pieces. Leave to dry.

Step 2

Using fine-grade sandpaper, lightly sand the surfaces of all the pieces. Mix some of the yellow ochre artists' acrylic colour with just enough water to 'loosen' the paint (see *Mixing glazes* on page 24), apply a coat of this to the pole and leave to dry.

Day Two

Step 3

Start 'plaiting' the pole with cord or string. A smooth and fairly broad cord is best because it will not slip so easily when applying the final colour. Pin the centre of the length of cord into one end of the pole, making two almost equal lengths. Wind one length in one direction as evenly as possible to the end. Then wind the second length, adjusting the spacing if required to keep the crossovers as consistent as possible along the pole.

Step 4

Mix some of the red ochre artists' acrylic colour with just enough water to 'loosen' the paint (see *Mixing glazes* on page 24). Apply this red ochre paint to the pole over the cord, and also to all the other pieces. Leave to dry.

Step 5

Remove the cord from the pole and put the pole aside.

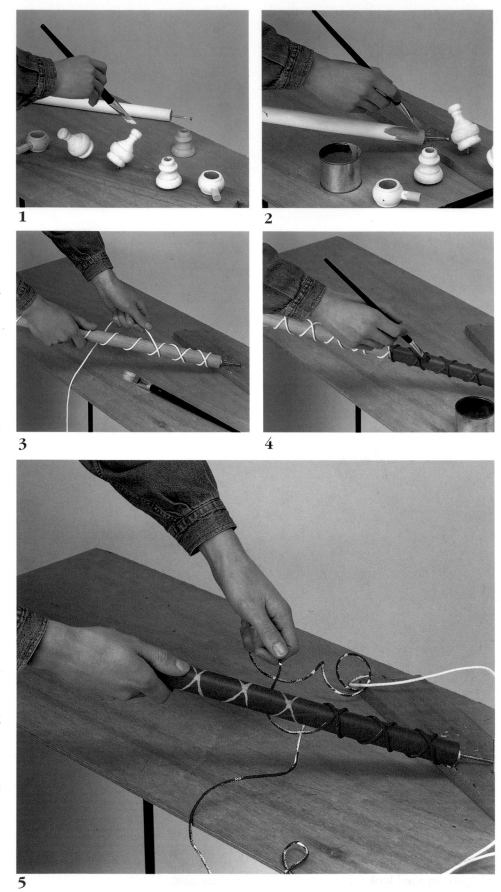

1

2

3

4

5

6

7

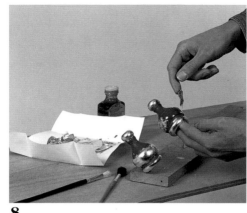

8

Step 6

Apply gold size to the surfaces to be gilded and leave for the time specified, according to the manufacturer's instructions and atmospheric conditions.

Step 7

Test if the surface is ready to gild by placing the back of your knuckle on it – it is ready if your knuckle pulls slightly but cleanly away, or if your knuckle makes a squeaking sound as it is pulled across the surface.

Step 8

Apply the leaf. I have used Dutch metal as it is much thicker than gold leaf (and significantly cheaper) and can be handled much more easily. Tamp the leaf down as you proceed.

Step 9

When dry, brush off excess leaf using a very soft brush across the actual surface of the leaf and using a stiffer brush where the edges meet the paint. Apply one or two coats of button polish to the Dutch metal to enrich the colour and to protect the gold from tarnishing.

Varnish all surfaces. Apply a dark or 'black' wax to all surfaces if required, and buff. This will enhance the colour and give an aged look.

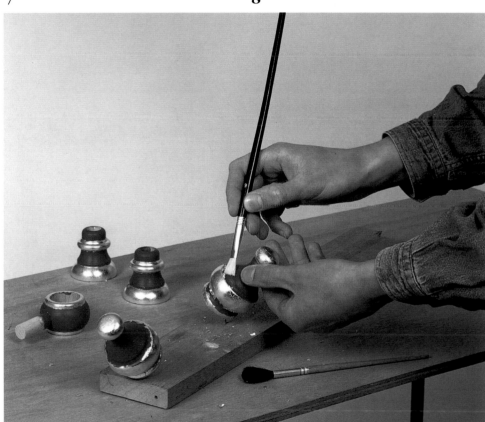

9

Painting rings and pole

Tie all the rings onto a length of string, leaving enough space between each so that they do not touch. Then pin or tie the string between supports, two chairs for example, for easy handling when sanding and painting and also while drying. With a bradawl, make a start hole at both ends of the pole and fit two long screws, inserting them just so far that they do not move around. The screws can then be rested between two surfaces and the pole worked on and painted, turned round and left to dry without damaging any of the wet surface paint.

Glazed and combed picture frame

New picture frames are expensive to buy, but an old frame can be restored and given a decorative paint effect to enhance a painting or print.

The restoration of picture frames is now accepted as an important part of the general care of the decorative arts. The frame is not just the structure that surrounds and supports the painting or print, it is a part of the whole effect. Without the right frame, a picture loses some of its character.

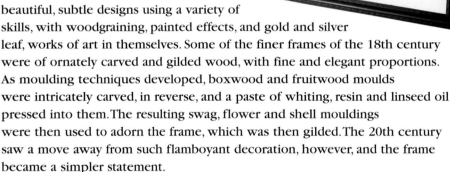

Any visit to a museum or art gallery will reveal the art of the picture framer. In the Renaissance period of the 14th and 15th centuries, framers produced beautiful, subtle designs using a variety of skills, with woodgraining, painted effects, and gold and silver leaf, works of art in themselves. Some of the finer frames of the 18th century were of ornately carved and gilded wood, with fine and elegant proportions. As moulding techniques developed, boxwood and fruitwood moulds were intricately carved, in reverse, and a paste of whiting, resin and linseed oil pressed into them. The resulting swag, flower and shell mouldings were then used to adorn the frame, which was then gilded. The 20th century saw a move away from such flamboyant decoration, however, and the frame became a simpler statement.

Painted finishes have always been popular. They are less expensive to produce and not as labour intensive as a gilded finish. Using the painting or picture as inspiration, the glazes and colours can be worked to great effect.

Planning your time

DAY ONE
AM: Sand and prepare surfaces; glue joints

PM: Apply all-in-one primer and undercoat; paint top colour

DAY TWO
AM: Mix glaze; apply and comb

PM: Varnish

Tools and materials

G-clamps

Length of cord

Panel pins

Hammer

Nail punch

PVA wood glue

Wood filler

Spatula

Medium and fine-grade sandpaper

Sanding block

All-in-one primer and undercoat paint

Paint for top colour

Artists' acrylic colours – yellow ochre, raw umber

Paintbrushes
(including dragging brush)

Jars for mixing paint

Comb (available from decorators' merchants) or card cut to shape

Varnish

Cloth

Scumble glaze (available from decorators' merchants)

1

2

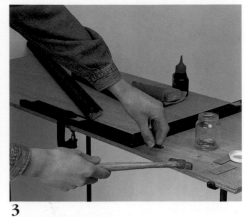

3

Day One

Step 1

Where joints are loose or the frame is coming apart, remove any nails or pins, then sand down the edges to remove old glue.

Step 2

Apply PVA wood adhesive to the sanded edges and position the frame on a flat surface.

Step 3

Tap panel pins across the corners, using a nail punch.

Step 4

When all the corners are pinned, leave the glue to dry, keeping the frame flat. Secure it with a rope tied all round the frame and tightened like a tourniquet, using a piece of dowelling. This prevents any movement in the joints while they dry. Fill any holes or cracks with wood filler, paying attention to the mitred corners. Sand down filled areas.

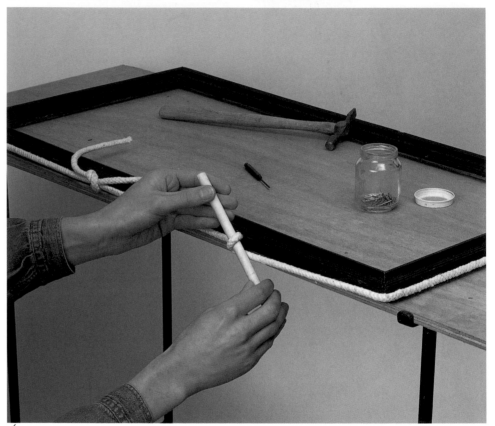

4

Using clamps

It can be a help when gluing and pinning the corners of the frame, particularly the first one, to have one side of the frame secured to the work surface with G-clamps. This will prevent it moving around when tapping in the pins. Use the clamps also when combing, but always remember to put something between the clamp and the painted surface, such as folded card or a thin piece of wood, to protect it.

5

6

7

8

Step 5
Apply all-in-one primer and undercoat and leave to dry. Apply top colour and leave to dry.

Day Two

Step 6
Mix up glaze colour (see *Mixing glazes* on page 24) and apply one section at a time, brushing out evenly. With the use of a comb, start working along in one direction all the way to the end, then go back, working in the opposite direction to make a criss-cross pattern.

Step 7
Wipe off the edges and mitred corners and work on the opposite side. When dry, do the remaining sides.

Step 8
Apply glaze to the edges and 'drag' a stiff brush through. Wipe off any overlaps. Leave to dry. Varnish all surfaces of the frame.

Combing
....

When combing on a concave surface, such as this frame, hold the comb straight and flat on the edge and, with an even pressure, draw it towards the body and slightly to one side. Using both hands on the comb will help to keep the pressure even. If the pattern goes wrong, simply brush out and start again.

Bookshelf unit

With the addition of a decorative cut-out, cornice and side pieces, a plain set of shelves can become an attractive and unique item to use for display.

There is always space in a home for an extra set of shelves. It sometimes seems that, no matter how much shelving there is, there are always more bits and pieces to fill the space than there are shelves to house them. The inspiration for this set of shelves came largely from an old dresser. Although completely different in its proportions, the decorative cut-out at the top works as well over the narrow width of this piece of furniture as it did on the original, much wider piece. As an alternative top section you could cut out a simpler shape in MDF (medium density fibreboard) and create a design by drilling holes to form a pattern using a large drill bit. You could drill a design in, for example, clover leaves or flower shapes.

The addition of the cornice to these tall, narrow shelves accentuates their height and weight. This technique would work equally well on a smaller set of shelves that could then be wall mounted.

By attaching a backing board all the way down, the 'interior' of the shelf unit could be decorated to contrast with the exterior paint. This could be a complementary colour or a textured finish such as a simple graining or dragged brush stroke.

Planning your time

DAY ONE
AM: Work out design, cut MDF and affix cut-out shape; cut and affix cornice and beading

PM: Apply primer and undercoat, after filling and sanding

DAY TWO
AM: Apply top coat of paint

PM: Apply finishing 'wash'

Tools and materials

Sandpapers

Sanding block

Wood filler

Spatula

All-in-one primer and undercoat

Paint for final colour

Artists' acrylic paints – raw umber, white

Varnish

MDF (medium density fibreboard)

G-clamps

Cornice (old pieces are sometimes available from reclamation yards)

Beading

Jigsaw

Pencil

Tracing paper

Tape measure

Hammer

Nail punch

Mitre box

Saw

Panel pins

Paintbrushes

Jars for mixing paint

Pieces of wood for fixing cornice

Screwdriver

Screws

Bradawl

Wood glue

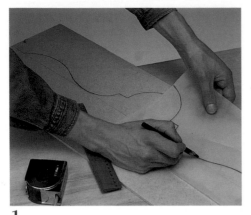

1

2

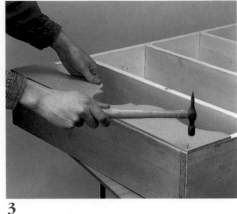

3

Day One

Step 1
Thoroughly sand down all the surfaces of the shelves, filling any holes as necessary. Plan your design for the cornice on tracing paper, then measure and mark it out on MDF (medium density fibreboard).

Step 2
Following your marked line, cut out the design using a jigsaw or ask a timber merchant to do so for you.

Step 3
Apply glue to the edges of the cut-out shape edges and fix it to the top of the shelves using panel pins.

Step 4
Measure the lengths required for the cornice and cut them with the aid of a mitre box, making the side pieces longer than required. Place the cornice pieces in position at the top of the shelf unit and draw a pencil line along the inner edge of the cornice. This will be the guideline for fixing blocks that are to be screwed onto the shelf unit.

4

Planning the design
To reproduce a symmetrical design, draw one half onto tracing paper. Transfer it to the surface to be cut, then simply turn the design over and follow the reverse shape to produce an accurate mirror image.

Step 5

Cut out five or so pieces of timber for the fixing blocks and drill a hole in each one for the screws. Fix the blocks to the cornice with glue and nails or panel pins. Position the front cornice section and use a bradawl to make the starter holes for the screws.

Step 6

Fit the side cornice sections, gluing the mitred joints. Saw off the excess cornice from the sides.

Step 7

Measure and cut lengths of beading for the side edges of the shelf unit. Glue and affix them to the side edges using panel pins with the aid of a nail punch. Fill in any gaps with wood filler and sand them down. To finish the 'base' of the shelf unit cut two small pieces of the cornice, turn them upside down, then pin and glue them in place, one on each side.

Step 8

Apply undercoat to the whole shelf unit and leave to dry. Apply the top coat of paint. Leave to dry.

Day Two

Step 9

Apply a wash of a very dilute white with a touch of raw umber. Brush out very well – this will 'soften' the overall colour and give a slightly powdery effect. Leave to dry, then varnish the whole shelf unit.

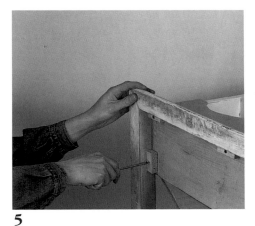

5

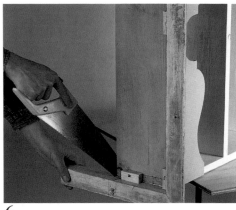

6

7

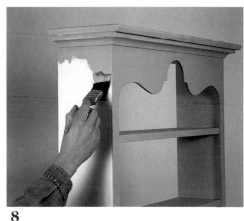

8

9

Scumble-glazed trunk

A smart scumble-glaze finish with a variety of decorative marks now allows this solid and spacious trunk to be put on show rather than hidden away.

As a practical piece of furniture in which to keep large, bulky items such as bedding and pillows, the blanket chest or trunk has had a long and useful life. Not only was it used for storing items in the home, it was also the forerunner to the suitcase and packing case, providing sturdy housing for the personal belongings of the traveller.

The shapes, sizes and finishes of such chests varied. Some were made from fine, rare timbers with lacquered finishes, while others were of basic, plain pine. Ships' trunks had brass corners and fittings to provide reinforcement and protection, while some communities who could not afford

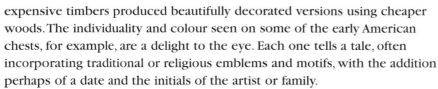

expensive timbers produced beautifully decorated versions using cheaper woods. The individuality and colour seen on some of the early American chests, for example, are a delight to the eye. Each one tells a tale, often incorporating traditional or religious emblems and motifs, with the addition perhaps of a date and the initials of the artist or family.

It is fun to play with glazes. Oil glaze will give a longer 'open' time in which to work the glaze, but it takes longer to dry. When using a water-based glaze, work on small areas at a time. Try using different tools and objects to create the effects – even fingers make interesting designs in the glaze!

If all four sides are decorated, this piece could easily be placed in front of a sofa as a coffee table while still being put to use as extra storage space.

Planning your time

DAY ONE
AM: Sand, fill, and prepare surfaces; mend the lid

PM: Paint the undercoat and undercolour

DAY TWO
AM: Apply the glaze and decorate

PM: Varnish

Tools and materials

Two lengths of timber (approximately 45 cm [17¾ in] required here)

Tape measure

Drill

Screws

Screwdriver

Medium and fine-grade sandpaper

PVA glue

Two-part resin wood filler

Bradawl

Spatula

Saw

A variety of paintbrushes

All-in-one primer and undercoat paint

Paint for top colour

Scumble glaze (available from an art suppliers)

Pigments or artists' acrylic paints – for example, red ochre or red oxide, olive green, burnt umber, yellow ochre

Items to make glaze patterns, such as card, combs (available from specialist decorators' merchants), corks, potatoes

Cloth

Jars for mixing paints and glazes

Varnish

Fine wire wool

Day One

Step 1

Remove the hinges from the lid. To assemble the parts of the lid assemble them on a flat surface. Using a sanding block, sand the edges of the lid that will be glued together. This removes any old glue as well as giving a clean, sharp edge to the pieces.

Step 2

Measure and cut two pieces of timber for reinforcing the lid and drill three or four holes in each. Apply glue to the edges of the lid pieces and push them together carefully.

Step 3

Using a bradawl through the holes in the reinforcing pieces, mark out the position of the screws on the lid.

1

2

3

Mending the lid

When measuring and cutting the reinforcing battens for the lid, make sure they are short enough to allow the lid to fit snugly when it is closed, allowing for the hinges and overlap.

4

Step 4

Apply glue to the underside of the reinforcing pieces and fix immediately in place with screws, making sure that all sections of the lid fit together properly. Leave to dry.

Step 5

Sand down all the surfaces of the trunk and fill any holes and gaps with a two-part resin wood filler, paying particular attention to where the lid has been glued together. When the wood filler is dry, sand the filled areas.

Step 6

Apply a coat of all-in-one primer and undercoat paint. Leave to dry.

5

6

Storing paints

To prevent mixed paints from drying out, either store them in jars with lids or use plastic food wrap secured with elastic bands. Acrylic paints dry out quickly when exposed to the atmosphere.

Step 7

Apply the top colour paint, which will be the base for the glaze work.

Day Two

Step 8

Mix the glaze with your chosen pigments. Apply the glaze and add the decoration to it in sections. Brush the mixed glaze and pigment onto the top and bottom edges first and use a decorators' comb to make the pattern.

7

Mixing glazes

The first stage is to mix up the concentrated colour required. Here artists' acrylic paints were mixed together in a jar. To this add acrylic scumble glaze – to start with add approximately half the volume of mixed colour in the jar. Blend thoroughly, adding a little water to 'loosen' it. Try out this mixture on a piece of paper or card, adding more glaze or water until the right tone is achieved. Too much water will cause the paint to run, and too little will make the glaze too thick and it will dry in ridges.

8

Step 9

Apply the glaze and pigment mixture to the sides of the trunk, one panel at a time. Make a pattern in the glaze by dabbing a potato cut in half into the glaze.

Step 10

Simply brush on the final colour with even strokes. Remember to wipe off the edges as you go along, before the glaze dries. Then leave the trunk to dry. Fix the lid back in place. Varnish all surfaces and again leave to dry. Distress the surface of the decoration lightly, if required, by rubbing over with fine wire wool, paying particular attention to the edges as they would receive more wear.

9

Storing mixed glazes and colours

When a coloured glaze is chosen, always aim to mix up a good quantity – it is better to have too much than not enough. Store the remainder in a jar with a lid to keep, should you need to retouch chipped areas at a later date.

Cleaning brushes

Brushes used for gold size, which is oil-based, should be cleaned in white spirit or turpentine. Brushes used for shellac products (for example, button polish), which are alcohol-based, should be cleaned in methylated spirits.

10

Sponged cot

A sponged design of elephants makes this a special bed for a special child. Any number of designs can be applied to furniture using this easy technique.

Planning your time

AM: Sand and prepare surfaces.
Apply undercolour paint

PM: Paint top colour

DAY TWO
AM: Apply sponge design

PM: Varnish

Tools and materials

Sandpaper

Wood filler

Spatula

All-in-one primer and undercoat

Top coat (or scumble glaze mixed
with various artists' colours)

Artists' acrylic colours – yellow
ochre, black

Kitchen sponges

Matchsticks

Scalpel

Scumble glaze

Paintbrushes, including a wide
flat one for 'dragging'

Flat dish for printing

Jars for mixing paint

Non-toxic varnish

The derivation of the word 'cot' is Anglo-Indian from the Hindi word 'khat'. Societies all over the world and throughout history have had a tradition of embellishing and personalizing their children's first bed. There are no boundaries when it comes to decorating a baby's or toddler's cot. It is an individual piece.

The basic creative ideas should come from imagining waking up to something that can charm, soothe or stimulate a young mind. Mass-produced and plain cots offer little, but by giving an individual touch to one you can make it special and personal – after all, every child is unique.

The technique of printing with sponges is very simple and almost any design can be adapted – geometric shapes, a whole jungle of animals, boats, stories in print. The only limits are having the patience to cut out the figures and a good supply of sponges!

Vegetable prints are also suitable – using half a potato and cutting out a design on it to stamp is a time-honoured way to make a simple decoration, but courgettes can be used in a similar way and hold the paint well.

Although this particular cot is traditional in design, providing large areas on which to print, this technique of printing can be applied to any style of bed or cot. Walls and floors can be given the same treatment, too.

Remember to check that the varnish you use is non-toxic.

1

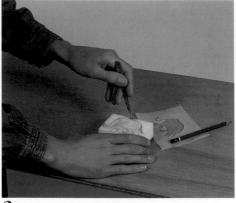

2

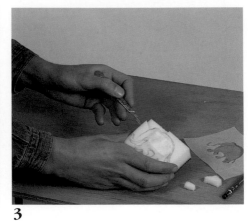

3

Day One

Step 1

Clean and sand all surfaces, using medium, then fine-grade, sandpaper. Fill any holes with wood filler, and sand. Apply an all-in-one primer and undercoat to any raw wood. When dry apply a second coat of all-in-one primer and undercoat, tinted with a small quantity of yellow ochre and a touch of black to make a soft 'off white'. Then apply the colour by 'dragging' the brush through the paint. This can be done with a very dilute, thin paint or by adding artists' colour to glaze.

Step 2

It is easier to apply the top colour in sections, allowing drying between sections and wiping off overlaps on the edges. While you are waiting for the paint to dry, you can work out the design for your sponge on tracing paper. Apply the design to the sponge by cutting around the paper and marking the outline on the sponge. Cut around the design with a scalpel or very sharp knife.

Step 3

Cut away the area of sponge around the outline, so that the design is standing proud.

4

Day Two

Step 4

Mix a quantity of colour in a jar and pour out onto a flat dish. Push the sponge design down into the paint and make sure that the pattern is evenly coated. You may wish to touch up some areas of the sponge with a brush. Then apply the sponge stamp firmly to the head panel of the cot.

Dragging

An ordinary, reasonably wide decorators' brush will do as an alternative to a dragging brush. As the strokes reach the lower edge, pull the brush back up briskly and vertically, 'fading' it off the surface – this avoids an ugly build-up of paint and an abrupt, untidy finish to the downward strokes.

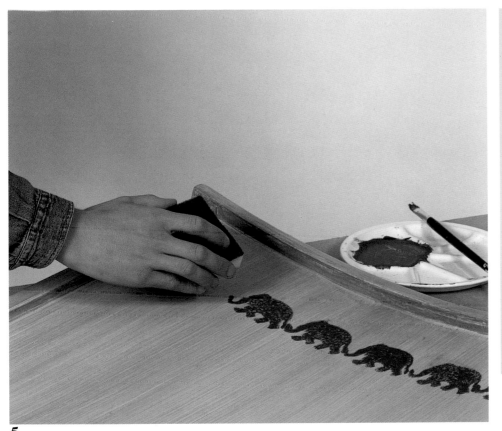

5

6

7

Using sponges

This printing technique uses synthetic sponges. It can also be applied to walls or fabrics, although if the fabric is to be washed use a fabric dye rather than paint and follow the manufacturer's instructions. When cutting out the design use a sharp craft knife or scalpel blade and work in reverse to the way it will be printed.

Step 5

Recoat the sponge with paint for each printed motif. Apply each print closely to the previous one and keep an even line, to make a linked row of elephants.

Step 6

Allow the first colour of printing to dry. Make futher small sponge cut-outs and overprint onto the elephants using a different colour of paint.

Step 7

When the second colour of printing is dry, overprint detail using the end of a matchstick and a third colour. Leave to dry, then varnish all surfaces with a minimum of two coats to protect your handiwork, making sure that the varnish is non-toxic.

Printing

You may wish to varnish the panels and leave them to dry before painting. When dry, draw a faint pencil guideline that can be removed later. Varnishing at this stage means that any misprints or mistakes can be wiped off easily without the risk of damaging the painted surface underneath. Use a hairdryer to speed up drying time for the overprinting.

Cottage door

The addition of studs and lengths of timber make this plain wooden door look as if it has stood at the entrance to your cottage for hundreds of years.

The most obvious comment to make about a door is that it is the first feature to be seen when entering a room and the last when leaving. So it makes an impression, however momentary that may be. There is nothing more uninspiring than a modern, fireproof, flat-panelled door, complete with aluminium latch handle, but it can be expensive and sometimes impractical to change the door for another one. Apart from cost, the frame may not be a standard size, so finding a door to fit may not be easy; or the replacement door may need planing down and adjusting for fit.

So, instead, look at ways of improving the existing door with the addition of mouldings to create panels that could then hold coloured glass, mirror or fabric. Change the aluminium handles for porcelain, brass or turned wooden ones, or simply apply a paint effect, such as graining or dragging, to the surface of the door. Adding a decorative architrave to surround the door will also enhance its character.

This door has been given a cottage-style treatment, the effect completed by a traditional latch door handle. The contrasting white surface with black studs and handle creates a striking combination. The overall effect fools the eye into believing that the door is heavy and strong when, in fact, the same lightweight door remains beneath the dressing. This is the art of illusion.

Planning your time

DAY ONE

AM: Remove handles; sand all surfaces and fill where necessary; cut timber, pin and glue; apply primer and undercoat

PM: Paint top colour; paint stud heads (if required)

DAY TWO

AM: Fix studs into place

PM: Fix new handle, drilling if required

Tools and materials

Sandpaper

Sanding block

Screwdriver

Drill

Stanley knife

G-clamps

Lengths of timber (12 x 20 mm [½ x ¾ in] in width and depth)

Wood filler

Spatula

All-in-one primer and undercoat

Tape measure

PVA wood glue

Panel pins

Hammer

Nail punch

Top colour paint – oil-based 'eggshell' used here

Studs

Spanner to fit studs

Latch door handle

Paintbrushes

White spirit (for cleaning)

Bradawl

Day One

Step 1

Remove the door and place it on a flat surface to work on. Remove the door handles from both sides. Sand down the door. Fill in any holes with wood filler, and then sand them. Measure out the lengths of timber required. Clamp the timber to a table or workbench using G-clamps. Then cut the top edges of the timber with a sharp craft knife to create a 'rough', uneven look.

Step 2

Very lightly sand the cut edges with fine-grade sandpaper to remove any splinters.

Step 3

Drill evenly spaced holes for studs in all the pieces of timber. Measure out the positions for the timber on the door. Run a line of PVA wood glue along the edges of the timber that will be placed on the door.

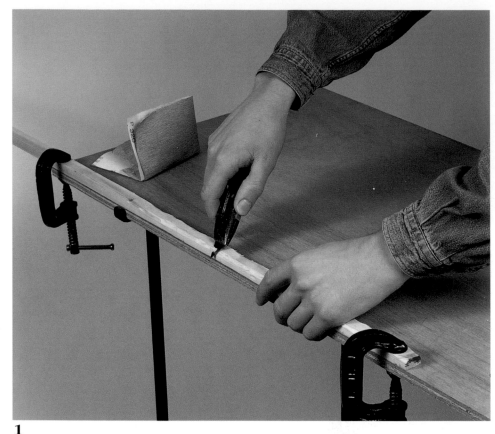

1

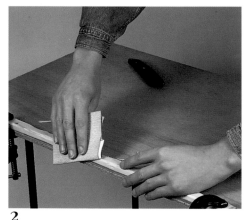

2

3

Planning the panels

Generally speaking, five panels are easier on the eye with this style of door (rather than four or six). Remember, when doing both sides of the door, that the timber uprights will need to be cut slightly shorter on one side if they are to fit against the door stop.

Cutting with a craft knife

As a safety measure always cut away from the body in case the knife slips, and keep the other hand well out of the path of the blade.

4

5

6

Step 4
Place the glued pieces of timber on the door. Affix them securely onto the door with panel pins in two or three places near the screw holes.

Step 5
Apply all-in-one primer and undercoat to all surfaces. Leave to dry. Apply the top coat of paint to all surfaces. Leave to dry.

Day Two

Step 6
Fix the studs into the door using a spanner if necessary.

Step 7
Position a new handle or latch on the door and, if required, drill for fitting through to the other side. Make a starter hole with a bradawl, then screw the handle into place.

7

Studs
If ready-made decorative door studs are not available, improvise by using plain metal wood studs and paint the tops with black enamel before fitting. If you are using a spanner to fit the studs, line the inside of the spanner head with masking tape to prevent it scratching the painted surface.

Decorated Lloyd Loom chair

The natural texture of Lloyd Loom furniture fits in well with modern furnishings. This old chair has been refurbished for a brand new look.

Lloyd Loom furniture, contrary to what most people believe, is neither cane nor wicker. In fact, it is made from a type of strong brown paper (Kraft paper) that is woven around steel wire. Its invention was due to Marshall B. Lloyd (1858–1927), a manufacturer of wicker prams in Michigan, USA. As wicker furniture became more and more popular, it became obvious to Mr Lloyd that the slow process of weaving by hand needed to be improved upon. His invention, in 1917, of the loom and the technique that made large-scale production viable revolutionized the industry and gave its name to the famous Lloyd Loom furniture.

In 1922 William Lusty and Sons Ltd of London acquired the rights to produce the furniture in England, and during the 1920s and '30s this style of furniture became very fashionable. Although originally marketed as a range of high quality garden furniture, Lloyd Loom soon became all the rage as pieces were bought for use indoors in bedrooms, bathrooms, studies; in fact any room where its versatility and elegant practicality proved its merit.

The furniture is still being produced, and surviving samples from the 1920s and '30s are much sought after in the antiques trade.

The piece worked on in this project had several coats of paint layered on top of the original. Stripping it down was not practical, so I applied paint and decoration by brush; spraying the paint onto the surface works very well too.

These techniques can also be applied to cane or wicker furniture.

Planning your time

DAY ONE
AM: Clean and prepare base and feet; apply undercolour

PM: Mask off design

DAY TWO
AM: Paint top colour

PM: Varnish

Tools and materials

Wire brush

Wire wool

Sandpapers

Undercolour paint – off-white or cream

Top overcolour paint – grey-blue

Masking tape

Tape measure

Paintbrushes

Varnish, mixed with a small quantity of artists' acrylic paint (raw umber) if required

1

Day One

Step 1
Using a wire brush, work vigorously over the whole surface of the chair to remove any flaking paint.

Step 2
Using fine-grade sandpaper, sand the chair as much as possible to key the surface. Then dust off using a soft brush, making sure that you clean out all the crevices. Finally, use a vacuum cleaner to make sure the weave is free of dust.

Step 3
Clean the paint off the feet of the chair with wire wool to reveal the original brass capping.

2

3

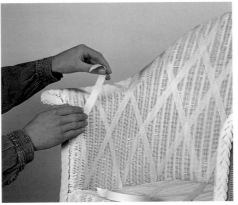

4

5

Step 4
Apply the undercolour paint to the whole of the chair, and leave to dry.

Step 5
Use masking tape to make a criss-cross pattern across the inside of the chair and over the seat. Measure the centre of the back of the chair and work outwards on either side. Make sure that the tape is well stuck to the surface.

Day Two

Step 6
Apply the top colour paint to the whole chair. Leave to dry. Remove the masking tape. Varnish all surfaces; a touch of raw umber artists' acrylic paint can be added to 'age' the finish if you wish.

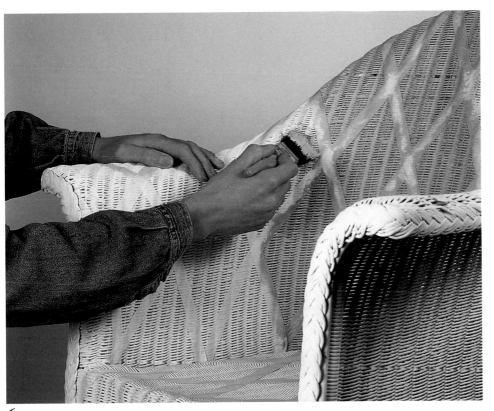

6

Stencilling
You could also use stencils, such as a fleur de lys design, to make a pattern. Cut out the design and mark it out on the chair, again working from the centre of the chair back. Use a brush or a sponge to apply the paint over the stencil. This technique can also be applied to cane furniture.

Japanned table

The sole survivor of a nest of tables has been japanned to create an attractive games or side table. The effect is easy to achieve.

The art of japanning was popular in the 18th century and was developed as a substitute for the real lacquered furniture of the Orient that originated in China over one thousand years ago. The art thrived well into the 19th century. Tinted shellac or varnish was applied to the prepared surface, building up the layers, and then decoration was applied.

True lacquer comes from the sap of a variety of Rhus tree, collected much as latex is collected from the rubber tree. The sap is processed and applied, usually to a wooden base, in a labour-intensive method of coating layer upon layer. Each layer is rubbed down with pumice stone, and clays and pigments are added to the lacquer until a fine, smooth finish is achieved, after which it is decorated.

Resin lacquer or 'lac' is a dark red, clear substance that comes from certain insects. It is heated to a liquid, sieved and cooled, then stored as flakes. Its distillation in alcohol produces shellac, which varies in depth of colour depending on its purity. It is applied to a gesso or plaster base and built up prior to decoration.

The table in this project has a gilded decoration applied to the surface of paint and shellac. The scattered flakes of leaf are based on the Japanese technique of 'hiramaki-e' (meaning 'flat, sprinkled picture'), the earliest examples of which date from the late 12th century. Silver leaf can also be used and if the flakes are placed in a paper cone you can control the flow more easily and accomplish intricate designs.

Planning your time

DAY ONE
AM: Cut and fit new timber; move top rail; sand and prepare surfaces; paint undercoat

PM: Paint several layers of black top colour

DAY TWO
AM: Apply gold size and leaf

PM: Apply shellac; wire wool and wax

Tools and materials

Medium and fine-grade sandpaper

Length of timber cut to size for side of table

Drill

Saw

Screws

Screwdriver

PVA wood glue

Wood filler

Spatula

All-in-one primer and undercoat paint (tinted with black)

Black top colour

Paintbrushes, including artists' brushes

Gold size (available from art suppliers)

Dutch metal (available from art suppliers)

Sieve

Stiffish bristle brush

White spirit (for cleaning)

Button polish

Brush (for button polish)

Methylated spirit (for cleaning)

'Black' wax

Soft cloth

Wire wool

Jars for mixing paints

1

2

3

Day One

Step 1

Clean and sand down all the surfaces of the table. Remove the front bar to disguise the fact that the table was originally part of a nest and to make it look more complete on its own.

Step 2

Replace the bar at the lower back, using screws to fix it.

Step 3

Measure and cut a piece of timber for the front and back. Glue the edges and screw the wood on, positioning it to match in with the sides. Fill in any holes or gaps with wood filler, allow to dry, and sand.

Step 4

Tint an all-in-one primer and undercoat paint with black and apply it to all surfaces, paying particular attention to the new wood.

Apply several coats of black paint. Allow each coat to dry, then use fine wire wool to sand down the surface between each, as a very smooth surface is required to create a lacquer effect. Clean off the dust each time with a soft cloth.

4

Sizing and gilding

When applying the gold size, use a soft brush and aim to keep the edges as straight and clean as possible – any area that is inadvertently sized will pick up the leaf whether it is wanted or not. To test the size for readiness to gild, place your knuckle on the surface and pull it directly away. It should make a clean 'tack' sensation if it is ready, slightly pulling at the skin, but not sticking. After laying the leaf, 'tamp' it down. You can use a soft brush for this and in some cases the edge of a clean finger or a 'pounce pad' made with a small piece of lint-free, fine-weave material (silk is perfect) padded tightly with cotton wool.

5

Step 5

Draw out the design for gilding. For a chequerboard, apply size to the solid squares first. When the size is ready (see *Sizing and gilding* on page 40) apply solid leaf (Dutch metal), tamp it down and brush away any excess.

For the speckled effect, apply gold size to the remaining squares. As the size becomes ready to gild, put a few pieces of leaf into a small sieve and, with a stiff brush used in a circular motion, rub the leaf through and onto the sized area.

Step 6

Tamp down firmly – I have used a pounce pad here. Remove any excess leaf with a soft brush.

Day Two

Step 7

Size along the outer edge of the table and gild, tidying up the edges afterwards. Apply two or three coats of button polish to the Dutch metal; this enhances the colour as well as protecting it. Cut back the high gloss with fine wire wool between the first and second coats, and on the final coat, leaving to dry between coats. Apply 'black' wax all over, and buff.

6

7

Paper collage screen

This old screen, originally covered with Victorian scraps, has been given a new lease of life with collage pictures made from magazine cut-outs.

Planning your time

DAY ONE
AM: Remove old canvas; fix new canvas and spray

PM: Paint canvas; cut out designs; paint top colour

DAY TWO
AM: Apply designs to the frames; varnish

PM: Fit braid

Tools and materials

Tack extractors

Scissors

Staple gun

Tape measure

Water sprayer

Paintbrushes

Paints

PVA glue

Quantity of coloured paper from magazines

Plain coloured paper (for example, wrapping paper)

Plain paper for templates

Strong paper glue (for example, border adhesive)

Varnish

Rubber solution glue

Braid

Quantity of calico (canvas)

Jars for mixing paint and glue

S ome of the most beautiful surviving screens are 17th century decorated lacquerwork pieces from the Coromandel coast of India. Their fate, sadly, was often to be cut down and made into mirror frames and cabinets, table tops and chests to satisfy a European market hungry for this style of decoration.

Since then, however, screens have been popular in all kinds of homes and buildings – from the grandest to the most humble. The Victorians loved to coat their screens with 'scraps' – small, coloured-paper images of flowers, bows, fruit and quaintly dressed children. The Arts and Crafts movement used contemporary fabrics and heavy, embossed papers. Screens are gaining in popularity again as pieces of furniture, but old ones are usually found in a very sorry state, requiring some care and attention.

A screen can be put to good use to break the monotony of a large wall, to enclose the seating area around the fire, to hide or disguise an unattractive feature in the room or simply on its own as a decorative feature, perhaps as a room divider. The decoration could be painted as a whole scene from one panel through to the next or, alternatively, découpage (paper cut-outs) could be applied.

1

Day One

Step 1
Remove the old canvas, and extract all old nails and tacks.

Step 2
Measure and cut out the new calico canvas and attach it to the frame with a staple gun (see *Stretching the canvas* below).

Step 3
Spray a mist of water over the new canvas and leave to dry. This 'stretches' the fabric, since it will tighten as it dries out again.

Stretching the canvas

It is much easier to staple the new canvas to the frame if it is lying flat. Make sure the weave is accurately vertical and horizontal, otherwise it will twist as it stretches. Start by stapling at the centres of the top and bottom edges, then similarly with the sides so that there is a diamond-like shape in the canvas. Then proceed from the centre outwards along the long sides, at regular intervals pulling the canvas as it is stapled but not so much as to cause a wrinkle at the edge. Do not staple quite up to the corners. Next, staple the top and bottom, again from the centre, fixing outwards, and finally do the corners. The diamond-shaped wrinkle should have disappeared.

2

3

4

Step 4

Seal the canvas by applying a size mixture made up of emulsion paint and PVA glue (use approximately one dessertspoon PVA to 2½ litres paint), diluted with water. Leave to dry. The screen will require at least two coats of this size mixture.

Step 5

Apply two to three coats of the background paint in the colour you have chosen for your frame. Leave to dry. Measure up and mark out the positions of the picture 'frames' on the screen.

Step 6

Cut out strips of plain coloured paper for the frames and glue them into position on the screen. You will need to use strong paper glue such as border adhesive or PVA.

5

6

7

Step 7

Work out the design on tracing paper, then transfer it to plain paper. Cut around the outline to provide a paper template. Cut out a template for each panel of the screen.

Step 8

Glue coloured papers onto the templates on the side to be seen, using border adhesive or PVA paper glue.

Step 9

When finished, turn to the reverse side of the designs and cut away the excess coloured paper overlapping the edges of the templates.

Leave the designs to dry between books to flatten them.

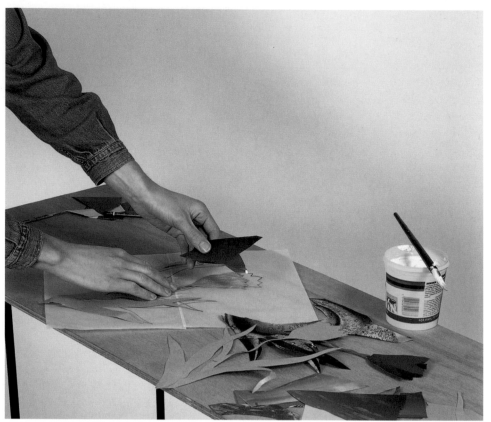

8

9

Decorating the screen

An alternative way to achieve a similar look for this screen, but without using collage, is to photocopy botanical prints. Tint the black and white photocopies by hand, cut the designs out and glue them into place.

Day Two

Step 10

Glue the designs in place on the panels. It helps to mark out the position first in pencil, say the top and bottom of each design. Leave to dry. Varnish all the panels and surfaces, and, again, leave to dry.

Step 11

Attach braid to the edges of the screen, using a rubber solution glue. Use thumbtacks to hold the folded mitred corners until dry.

10

Using upholstery studs

Upholstery studs, which come in a variety of shapes and sizes and are available from upholstery suppliers, could be used instead of glue to attach the braid to the frame. This will create an extra decoration on the border.

11

Mosaic garden table

A rusty metal table need not be thrown on the scrapheap. Painted and given a new mosaic surface, it becomes an attractive and useful piece of garden furniture.

The art of applying small pieces of clay, glass or stone to a surface has been practised for thousands of years. The inspiration for this technique probably came from the peoples of the early ancient civilizations who inlaid their ceremonial and religious objects with precious and semi-precious stones. The Ancient Romans perfected the craft and used pictorial mosaics extensively to decorate the floors and walls of their buildings.

The intricacy and individuality of mosaic work has kept its appeal, not just for its visual aspect but also as a practical and hardwearing surface. Some surviving examples of mosaic work date back to around 3000BC, and the exquisite designs of the Roman Empire still remain in excellent condition. Mosaics were largely applied to walls and floors in subtle tones of natural stone, but brighter glass mosaics were gradually introduced as far back as 200BC.

There are several methods for laying mosaic. This project uses one of the simplest and, although it is time consuming, it is fun to do and worth the effort. Mosaics can be applied to a variety of surfaces and objects, including terracotta pots, boxes, and frames, as well as walls and floors.

The more intricate the design, the smaller the pieces of tile will need to be and you might find a pair of mosaic nippers would be a useful addition to your tool kit. For a first attempt, aim to keep the design flowing and simple.

Planning your time

DAY ONE

AM: Prepare base and apply undercoat; cut out plywood top; apply primer sealer to top; drill holes in table top

PM: Attach new top

DAY TWO

AM: Apply oil-based paint to base; work out design and apply mosaic

PM: Grout top and leave to dry; clean off residual grout

Tools and materials

Drill

Dome-headed screws – chrome or zinc-plated

Waterproof plywood

Jigsaw

Wire brush

Coarse grit aluminium oxide abrasive paper (optional)

Paintbrushes

Quick-drying anti-rust primer paint

Primer sealer paint

Oil-based paint for final colour (eggshell or satin finish used here)

White spirit (for cleaning)

Tile cement or grout

Spreader

Dry pigments to tint grout – raw umber and black

Glass mosaics (available from specialist suppliers or, sometimes, tile merchants)

Paper for design

Sponge

Scourer

Screwdriver

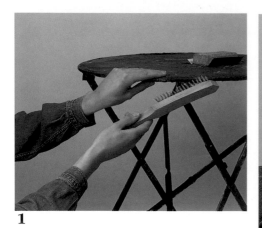

1

Day One

Step 1
Vigorously brush the base of the table with a wire brush to remove flaking pieces of rust. You could also use a very coarse grit aluminium oxide abrasive paper.

Step 2
Apply anti-rust primer paint to all surfaces with a paintbrush.

Step 3
Measure the top of the table and cut out a new one from waterproof plywood or similar wood using a jigsaw, or ask a timber merchant to do this for you. Apply primer sealer paint to both sides of the new table top. Leave to dry. Drill four or five holes in the metal top.

2

3

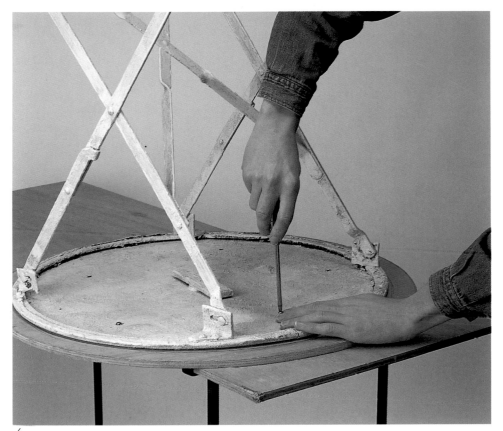

Step 4

Position the wooden top and attach it with screws from underneath through the drilled holes in the metal table.

Day Two

Step 5

Paint the base and underside with the final colour. I have used oil-based paint here as it is harder wearing, although it takes longer to dry.

4

5

Drawing a circle

Secure a piece of string with a drawing pin in the centre of the plywood and attach a pencil at the required length of radius. Then simply draw out the circle with the pencil.

Step 6

Meanwhile, work out the mosaic design and sketch it out on the new top. Sort out the mosaics into their colours and start applying the individual tiles to the top, putting tile cement on each. Overlap the mosaic tiles on the edge so that the ones on the vertical plane will make a right angle with those placed horizontally. Leave to dry, according to the manufacturer's instructions.

Step 7

Grout the tiles, making sure that all the areas are filled. Pigments can be used to tint the tile cement – here a small amount of raw umber and black is added to the cement.

6

Fixing the mosaics

Tile cement, although waterproof, is not as hard-wearing as mortar cement, but this takes approximately four days to cure or harden completely.

To obtain a perfectly flat surface to the mosaic tiles, stick them upper-face down, with a mild, water-soluble glue, onto paper following the required design. Then reverse the sheet onto a bed of cement. The paper can then be moistened with water and peeled off when the cement is dry. Then grout between the tiles.

7

8

Step 8
Wipe off the excess grout with a damp sponge and leave to dry.

Step 9
Any residual grout can be removed with a dampened scourer.

9

Fixing brass edging

As an alternative finish to the edge of the table, instead of using mosaic tiles, pin a strip of brass around. (This is available cut to size from engineers' suppliers.) Left to the elements, it will soon age (oxidize) naturally to take on the softer tones of old brass.

Folk art chest

This simple and charming effect for a small chest of drawers painted in a Folk Art style is based on a European design from the 19th century.

O ften found lurking in a spare room or garage, a flea market or a junk shop, a 1950s utility chest of drawers, heavily covered with several layers of gloss paint, can soon be transformed. With its utility ancestry disguised through the use of a muted colour scheme, simple decoration and distressing techniques, and with the addition of new handles, this small chest can become a classic piece of furniture. If the construction and style of the chest permits, you could also add feet and paint them to match the rest of the chest.

The charm of folk painting is in the personal touch. The detail created by the artist makes each piece an individual statement, and its colour and lyrical style adds life to any room or hallway. There is little formality or grandeur with this tradition of decoration when compared with the elegance of English and French painted furniture of the 18th and 19th centuries, or the highly adorned Italian pieces. But there is now renewed interest and enthusiasm worldwide for the simple and spontaneous style of Folk Art and its applications.

These decorative techniques can be equally applied to other pieces of furniture such as blanket chests, wardrobes or cabinets, and the colours selected according to your own schemes and the style of your home.

Planning your time

DAY ONE
AM: Remove old handles; cut and fit moulding; fill; sand and prime
PM: Apply undercoat colour; apply main colour; practise line painting and decoration

DAY TWO
AM: Paint decoration
PM: Distress with wire wool; add ageing coat

Tools and materials

Filler
Medium and fine-grade sandpaper
Sanding block and length of dowelling to suit curve of moulding
Mitre box and saw
Screwdriver
Drill or bradawl
Small-headed hammer
Small-headed nail punch
Panel pins
2 lengths of wood to raise chest off floor when painting
Various soft cloths
Sugar soap
Ruler (if required) for lining
Tape measure
Pencil
G-clamps
Length of moulding
Fine-grade wire wool
250 mm (1 in) and 375 mm (1½ in) bristle decorators' brushes
Artists' brushes
Varnish (satin or matt)
PVA glue
Acrylic quick-drying combined undercoat and primer for new wood
Top colour
Pigments (or artists' acrylics) – raw umber, French ultramarine and yellow ochre
Red ochre and white artists' acrylic colours for decorations

Day One

Step 1

Remove the old drawer handles. Take out each drawer to work on separately. Using sandpaper with a sanding block, thoroughly sand down all surfaces to remove any irregularities in the paintwork. Start with a medium-grade paper and finish with fine grade. The sanding also gives a key to which the next layer of paint can adhere.

Step 2

Cut the moulding with the aid of a mitre box and saw. Lightly sand the cut edges of the moulding first, then attach it to the top of the chest using panel pins, sinking them just below the surface with the use of a nail punch.

Step 3

Fill the holes left by the old drawer handles with wood filler and any gaps where the moulding is not flush with the body of the chest. Also fill in where pins have been sunk and any gaps in the mitred joints. Sand all filled areas when they are dry. Lightly sand the new moulding using sandpaper over a piece of dowelling.

Fix new handles. This may require drilling holes in the drawers – remember to countersink the screw on the inside of the drawers. Some handles come with a screw fitting attached – in this case make a small hole first in the surface of the drawer using a bradawl; the handle can then be screwed straight in.

Prepare all new wood (the moulding and handles) and filled areas by applying a combined acrylic primer and undercoat paint as this is quick drying. When dry, lightly sand with fine sandpaper, taking care not to be too harsh on the edges or the new exposed wood. Wipe down all surfaces with a soft cloth and sugar soap solution. This will clean away any sanding dust and remove any grease. Dry with another

1

2

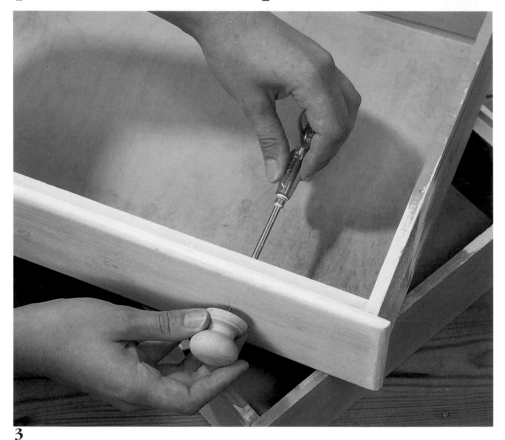

3

soft cloth. Raise the chest slightly off the ground, resting it on two lengths of wood, thus avoiding brushing grit or dust into the paint.

Step 4

Make up the undercoat colour by first mixing together some French ultramarine blue and a little yellow ochre artists' acrylic paint in a jar, then gradually add the acrylic primer and undercoat until fully mixed and the required colour and quantity obtained (about 900 ml [1½ pt] is plenty). Apply the paint to all surfaces – two coats are recommended, allowing drying time between each.

When the undercoat is dry, paint all the surfaces with the main colour. Apply the paint evenly in the direction of the wood grain underneath – generally speaking, from top to bottom on the sides and left to right on the top. Do not forget to paint inside the drawers.

4

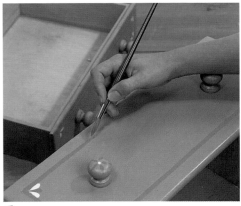

5

Day Two

Step 5

When all the paint is dry start the line painting and decoration. It is as well to practise this first on some sample board to perfect your technique and to work out your design. Leave to dry.

Step 6

Distress and age the piece using fine wire wool or fine-grade flour paper, working all over the surfaces and paying particular attention to the edges where there would be more wear. This also gives a key for the ageing wash. Dust down the chest of drawers, then mix together some raw umber pigment or acrylic paint and PVA glue diluted with a little water – just enough water to make the mixture brushable, but not too much that it will not adhere. Paint this all over the chest, concentrating on the areas that would collect more 'dirt' – around the drawer handles, in the moulding, and at the base. Before it is dry take a soft, dry cloth and with a dabbing action remove and blend the brush strokes and create a contrast, with some areas wiped clean. When dry, apply one or two coats of varnish.

6

Lining

If possible avoid using masking tape. Be confident and bold – a hand-painted line looks much softer. It is always worth using good quality brushes as a poor brush gives poor results and is frustrating and time wasting, particularly if you are a novice. Rest your little finger against the edge of the drawer as a guide or use a ruler tilted upwards.

Bronzed mirror

This old mirror, with much of its reflective surface peeling off, still retains its character and elegance with its frame newly decorated to give a bronzed effect.

Mirrors come in all shapes and sizes, from the purely functional to the richly adorned. Reflecting not just the image but also light, a mirror that is positioned well in a room can be as important a feature as a piece of fine furniture.

Over the centuries the mirror frame has had virtually every decorative technique possible applied to it, sometimes to the point where the glass is barely visible. Before the discovery of gas and electricity sconces were added to frames, projecting the reflected light of the candles. Convex, gilded mirrors, popular in the early 19th-century Regency period, had gilded balls surrounding the frames to amplify the brightness. Columns, shells and flowers added a further dimension to the flat expanse of glass. Frames were inlaid with mother of pearl and ivory. They were made of lacquered wood or beaten metal. The list of materials used to make and decorate mirror frames is endless.

The individuality and variety of styles is an inspiration in itself. The technique used here, with draped fabric and plaster of Paris, aims to produce a cast bronze that has oxidized to give a verdigris effect. Alternatively, the frame could be painted to look like stone, marble, or even gilded.

There are now suppliers of 'antiqued' glass, so an empty frame could be given the same treatment, with glass cut to size and fitted.

Planning your time

DAY ONE
AM: Work out design and cut out backing board; prime and seal surfaces and apply undercoat

PM: Mix up plaster of Paris and apply fabric design

DAY TWO
AM: Apply paint decoration

PM: Finish and wax; fix hanging fittings

Tools and materials

Backing board such as plywood or MDF (medium density fibreboard)

All-in-one primer and undercoat paint

Fittings for hanging (wire and rings)

Masking tape

Cloth (a piece of an old sheet will do)

Screws for fixing backing board

Plaster of Paris (available from potters' suppliers)

Whisk

Bucket and water for mixing

Scales

Measuring jug

Rubber gloves

Bronze powders

Artists' acrylic paints – burnt umber, phthalo green or viridian, raw umber, white

Paintbrushes

'Black' wax

Glass scraper or cleaner

Paper or lightweight card

Jars for mixing paint

Day One

Step 1

Clean and sand down the frame ready for undercoating. Lay the mirror onto the backing board being used, and work out the shape to cut out. Arrange the pieces of fabric to plan the design and to get the hang of folding fabric, and where to place the supporting cones and scrolls of paper. Draw around the design and frame on the board to give a guide for cutting.

Step 2

Cut out the backing board shape with the help of a jigsaw or ask a timber merchant to do this for you. Use screws to fix the new back to the mirror frame. Mask off the glass to protect against paint and plaster splashes. Apply a coat of primer paint to raw surfaces and undercoat to the whole frame.

Mix up plaster of Paris according to the manufacturer's instructions.

Step 3

Dip fabric into plaster of Paris, coat thoroughly and immediately place in position and fold into shape. Do not try and do the whole design in one go – work on each piece of fabric separately. Leave overnight to dry thoroughly.

1

2

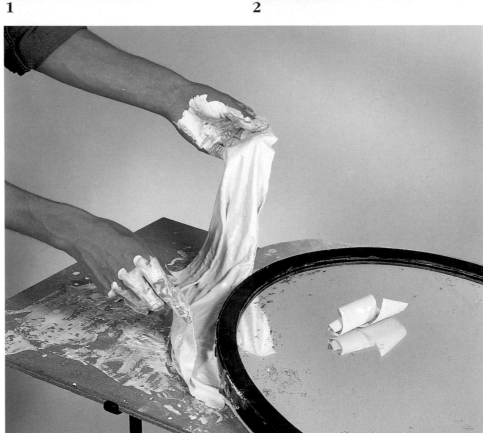

3

Using plaster of Paris

When mixed with an equal volume of water, plaster of Paris sets fairly quickly and becomes hard after anything from five to ten minutes. It hardens best in a dry atmosphere. This means working time is short, so it is worthwhile having a practice run with the fabric first to get the feel of it. Alternatively, there are ready-mixed plasters available that have slower setting times.

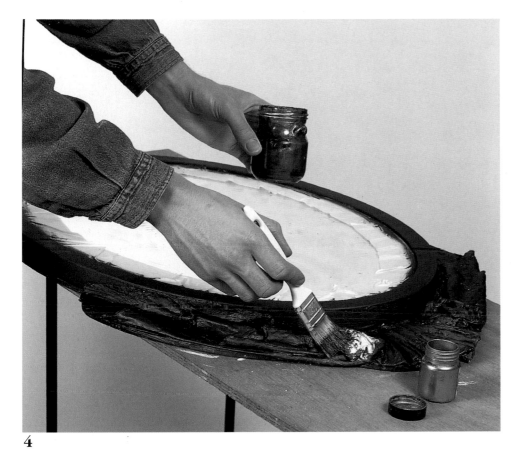

4

5

6

Day Two

Step 4

Paint a layer of 'bronze' onto all areas, by mixing some bronze powders with burnt umber acrylic paint in roughly the proportions of a quarter to a third volume powders to paint. Leave to dry.

Step 5

Apply 'verdigris' by mixing approximately equal amounts of white and raw umber paint to phthalo green (or viridian). Dilute with water. Cover the surfaces fairly liberally, making sure the paint gets into the folds and crevices. Soften immediately by dabbing with a soft cloth.

Step 6

Before the 'verdigris' dries completely, wipe off the top surfaces with a soft cloth so that these retain more of the 'bronze' colour. Leave to dry. Varnish or finish with 'black' wax on the top surfaces and buff with a cloth to bring out the bronze. Remove the masking tape and clean the mirror with a scraper if needed. Fix fittings to the backing board for hanging.

Fixing backing board

Use screws to attach the backing board to the frame of the mirror as, in the event of the glass getting broken, the back will be easy to remove and replace.

Wooden chair

Even an ordinary old wooden chair can be transformed successfully into an interesting piece. A bright cushion adds comfort and style, making the chair useful once more.

Van Gogh painted them; the Egyptians coated them in beaten gold and lapis lazuli; they were inlaid with semi-precious stones and mother of pearl in India; royalty had them padded, upholstered and raised up high; the Shakers hung them on walls. Chairs – all alike in one form or another – some to be sat on, some to be perched on uncomfortably, some really only to be looked at. The basic design – four legs and a back – has never stopped being designed, copied, reproduced, mass-produced and, more often than not, eaten away to a shaky end by woodworm (unless, of course, it's metal!).

It is extraordinary how layers of thick, white gloss paint so cleverly disguise the finer points of a piece of furniture, making it appear flat and unattractive. Usually, the paint has been applied with little or no preparation, straight on top of the layers underneath which, in turn, rest precariously and directly on top of the original shellac coating. This means that the paint, through age, becomes brittle and is relatively easy to 'flick' off right down to the shellac and wood.

Planning your time

DAY ONE
AM: Remove seat and any tacks or nails; strip off paint; clean with wire wool and methylated spirit

PM: Stain wood

DAY TWO
AM: Apply shellac, wire wool and wax

PM: Make box cushion

Tools and materials

Tack/nail extractors

Variety of scrapers

Methylated spirit

Wire wool

Cloth

Rubber gloves (if required)

Two-part resin wood filler

Fine abrasive paper

Woodstain

White polish (shellac without colour)

'Black' wax

Panel pins

Plywood for new seat

Foam for cushion

Brown paper

Pencil

Fabric for cushion

Piping cord

Pins

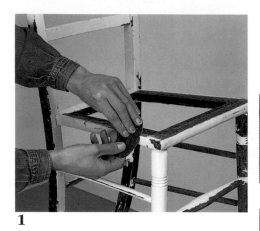

1

2

Day One

Step 1
Remove seat panel and extract any
tacks or nails. Start stripping the chair. If
the old paint 'pings' off easily with a
sharp tool or scraper, it is worth
persevering with this method (dry
stripping) as it is less messy than
chemical stripping. You could also use a
hot air gun.

Step 2
Clean the surface thoroughly with
methylated spirit and wire wool, wiping
off occasionally. This will remove the
old shellac. Fill any ugly holes left by
old nails or tacks – use a proprietary
resin wood filler as this will stain
better. Leave to dry.

Step 3
Apply woodstain with a soft cloth or a
brush, working systematically all over,
giving a second coat if required.
Leave to dry.

3

4

Day Two

Step 4
Apply several coats of clear, white polish, leaving to dry well between coats.

Step 5
Rub down with wire wool between the second and third coats of white polish and on the final coat.

5

Filling woodworm holes

Rather than using a filler that requires sanding and colouring, use a hard filler-wax (available from a timber merchant). This wax comes in several colours to match different woods. Press the wax into the holes with a spatula or similar, smoothing as you go. Do this prior to the final wax and buff finish.

Step 6

Apply wax ('black' wax is used here) with a brush or soft cloth. Then buff to a rich sheen.

Step 7

Measure the chair seat, and cut a piece of plywood to form a new base. Pin into place with panel pins. Buy a piece of foam pre-cut to the size that you require for the cushion. Place the foam on a sheet of brown paper and draw around it to make a paper pattern for the top and bottom of the cushion. You will need two of these. Then measure the depth and around the circumference of the foam. Transfer these measurements onto the brown paper to make a pattern for the side strip of the box cushion. Cut out the patterns and pin these three pieces onto your fabric.

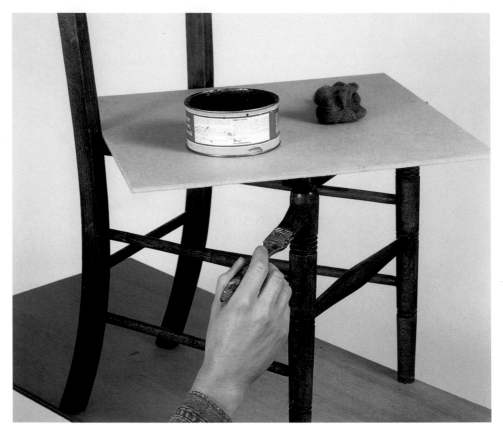

6

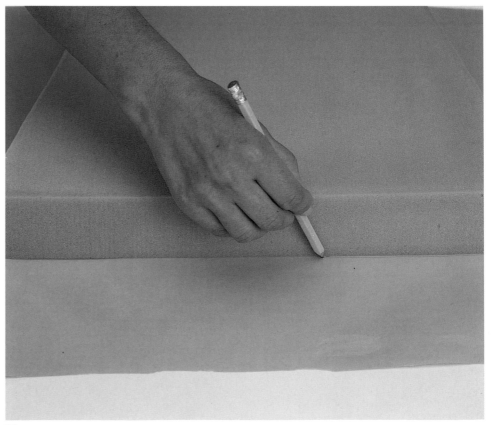

7

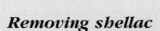

Removing shellac

Because methylated spirit dissolves shellac, this is a messy task and rubber gloves should be worn, not only to protect against staining the hands, but there may be some reaction in sensitive skins. The room should be kept well ventilated. Also, therefore, clean shellac brushes in methylated spirit.

9

8

Step 8

Cut out the top, bottom and side strip for the cushion, allowing a 2.5 cm (1 in) seam allowance. If you are using patterned fabric, make sure that you match the pattern on the side strip with that on the cushion top.

Step 9

To make the casing for the piping cord, cut 5 cm (2 in) wide strips, diagonally across the grain of the fabric. You will need enough piping to go round the cushion top piece of fabric.

Step 10

Join the strips for the piping on the diagonal, right sides together, and press the seams open.

10

11

12

Step 11

Place the piping cord on the wrong side of the long strip of fabric. Fold the fabric over to encase the cord and pin in place. Using a piping foot, machine stitch through the two layers of fabric as close as possible to the cord, securing it in place.

Step 12

To make the four ties for the back of the cushion, cut out four strips of fabric, 25 x 6 cm (10 x 2½ in). Press in half lengthways, wrong sides together, then press under a small turning along both long sides and one short side. Pin and baste these edges, leaving the other short end open. Machine stitch close to the turned edges and press. Repeat for each of the ties.

Step 13

Pin the piping all around the edge of the cushion top on the right side of the fabric, matching the edges of the fabric and with the bulk of the piping cord facing inwards. Where the ends of the piping meet, taper them into the seam line. Machine stitch, using the piping foot, taking care to catch in the ends of the piping securely. Trim these ends neatly and clip the seam, especially at the corners.

13

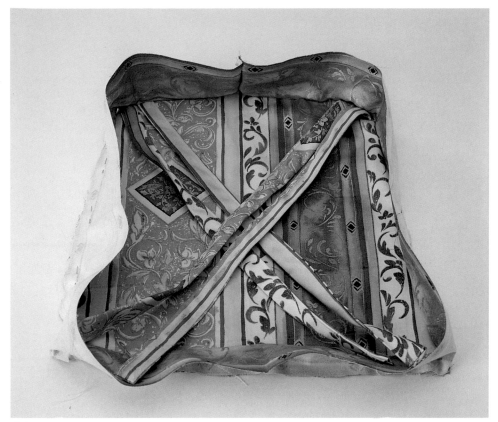

Step 14

Pin and machine stitch together the two short ends of the side strip, right sides together. Open out the seam and press. Pin together the fabric for the cushion bottom and side strip, right sides together, inserting two ties at each of the back corners. Put the piece of foam into the cover and try it on the chair to make sure that it fits. Remove the foam and machine stitch the fabric together, leaving a gap at the back to insert the foam later.

Step 15

Pin the piped cushion top to the side strip, right sides together, positioning the corners directly above those on the cushion bottom. Baste and machine stitch together. Clip the seam edges as before, then turn right sides out. Insert the foam cushion pad into the cover and oversew the opening.

14

15

Basting

If you are used to sewing, you will probably be able just to pin together sections of fabric before machine stitching them, thereby reducing the time taken on each seam by omitting the basting stage. But, if you are a complete beginner, it is easier to baste seams first. A little extra time spent at this stage will be worth it if it saves you unpicking wobbly seams later. If you do decide not to baste, sew over the pins very slowly, so as not to damage the machine needle, removing each pin as you come to it.

Freestanding kitchen cabinet

A fresh look at this serviceable, but rather dowdy, freestanding kitchen cabinet has turned it into a useful and stylish piece of furniture once more.

Planning your time

DAY ONE
AM: Sand and prepare surfaces; paint colour

PM: Apply design to aluminium panels

DAY TWO
AM: Apply panels; cut beading; prime and paint beading and new handles

PM: Fix beading and handles; varnish

Tools and materials

Hammer

Screwdriver

Nail punch

Panel pins

Drill

New handles

Medium- and fine-grade sandpaper

24 gauge (0.6 mm) aluminium sheeting (available from engineering suppliers)

Half-round beading

Mitre box and saw

Paintbrushes

Scumble glaze (from art suppliers)

Artists' colours or ready-mixed acrylic paint

Primer undercoat

Filler and spatula

Polyurethane varnish – satin finish

Ruler and coloured pencil

Bradawl

Jars or tins for mixing paint

G-clamps

Until fairly recently the kitchen was usually treated simply as a functional room in which to prepare food and keep the cleaning equipment. While an important part of the home, it was not decorated with the same attention to detail, style and colour as, say, a living room. However, these attitudes have changed and many now regard the kitchen as the heart of the home, often designing the kitchen as a room in which to eat and sit in comfort while still retaining its practical characteristics. The fitted kitchen with matching cupboards and cabinets, and a variety of accessories, is a relatively new concept. There are now many design companies specializing in kitchen furniture. Custom-made units are expensive, however, and while some off-the-shelf versions are more reasonable in price, it is nevertheless a costly

business to replace them when they are perfectly functional but not particularly attractive to look at.

This cabinet, which will be familiar to many people, with its harsh blank surfaces, can easily be transformed with the application of a little colour and a few simple techniques. New added panels change the dimensions of the doors. Various materials could be used for these panels, apart from aluminium sheeting, and teamed up with a wide choice of handles made from ceramics, brass, wood or glass.

1

Day One

Step 1

Remove handles and doors for working
·on a flat surface. Fill holes left by the
handles. Thoroughly sand all the
surfaces to be decorated. Mark out the
area to be panelled. Apply the
background colour or glaze. Brush it
out evenly and then 'drag' a broad flat
brush through the glaze, working in
sections following what would be the
direction of wood were the doors made
of timber. Wipe off clean straight edges
at the 'joins' and do not forget to paint
the edges of the cabinet. Leave to dry.
The colour used here was ready mixed
and then added to the scumble glaze
with a little water.

Step 2

Work out the design for the panels and
apply to the 'back' of the aluminium
sheets with a coloured pencil.

Step 3

With the pointed nail punch held
vertically, tap the head with the
hammer and work along the pencilled
guidelines, leaving approximately a nail-
punch distance between each punch
mark. This can be varied according to
your design.

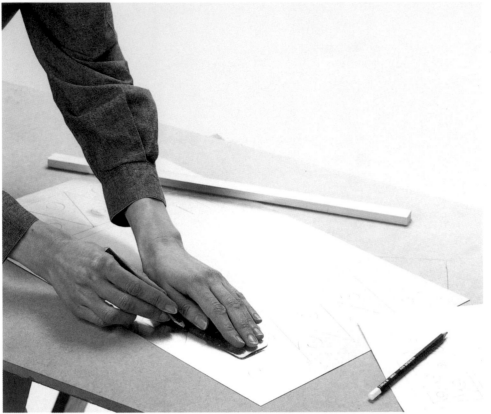

2

3

4

Step 4
Measure the lengths of beading for the panels and cut them using a mitre box and saw.

Day Two

Step 5
Paint primer undercoat on the beading and the new handles. Leave to dry. Apply the top colour and, again, leave to dry.

5

Punching the aluminium panels

Do not carry out this work on a good table as the punch may mark the surface. If necessary place a sheet of hardboard underneath the metal and clamp them both to the work surface to avoid it moving around while punching.

Step 6
With a bradawl make holes on the outer edges of the panels (for example, the corners and one or two per side).

Step 7
Position the panels on the doors and pin them into place using a flat nail punch and hammer.

6

Making mitres

When using the mitre box, either screw it to the work surface, if this is possible, or use G-clamps to secure it.

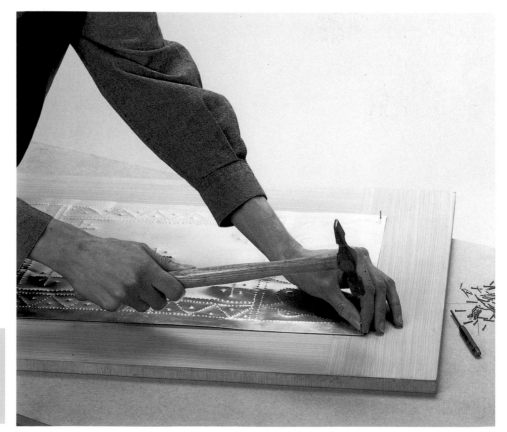

7

9

10

8

Step 8
Position the beading around the panels, overlapping the edges just enough to conceal the panel pins applied in Step 7, but allowing the beading pin to be tapped into the door itself.

Step 9
Drill holes for new handles and fix them into place.

Step 10
Apply two coats of polyurethane varnish to the painted surfaces, allowing drying time between coats. Mask off the panels to do this if necessary. Reassemble the unit when the varnish is dry.

Glossary

Artists' brushes

G-clamps

Dutch metal

Nail punch

Ageing and distressing
A technique using fine wire wool and/or flour paper (very fine abrasive paper) to rub through areas that would get naturally worn, followed by layer on layer of tinted varnish.

Artists' brushes
Finer tipped than decorators' brushes, these are used for detailed painting. They are available in a variety of sizes and qualities of hair, the most expensive being pure sable.

Black wax
A very dark wax used to give age and richness of colour.

Bradawl
A tool to make a small hole in wood prior to fixing with panel pins, nails or screws. Using a bradawl prevents the wood splitting.

Brushing out
Smoothing out uneven layers or brush strokes of paint or glazes.

Button polish
A type of shellac varnish, deriving its name from the small button-like shape of resin flakes that are then distilled in alcohol. It is a yellow or orange colour.

To countersink
To allow the screw to fit just below or flush with the surface, sometimes with the use of a countersinking tool.

Craft knife
A very sharp cutting knife with replaceable, and preferably retractable, blades.

Cutting back
Using fine wire wool or flour paper to reduce the sheen of paint or varnishes.

Decorators' brush
Broader and coarser than artists' brushes, decorators' brushes are usually bristle and for painting larger surfaces. They are available in a variety of widths and sizes.

Door fittings
This term usually refers to handles or latch handles, but also includes hinges, hooks etc.

Dry stripping
Removal of brittle layers of paint or varnish with the use of a fine, hard-edged tool or scraper. Useful when chemical stripping may damage the layer underneath.

Dutch metal
A metal alloy leaf, looking like gold leaf but which will tarnish with time if left unprotected – unlike gold. Available from art suppliers.

Filling woodworm holes
There is a variety of ways, from proprietary fillers to hard waxes.

Float a glaze
Where a reasonably dense layer of glaze is laid on the surface and pigments applied and softened. Used in paint techniques such as tortoiseshell marbling.

G-clamp
A tool to hold pieces of wood together while gluing; or to hold a piece secure to a work surface while working on it.

Jigsaw
A saw that allows elaborate shapes and curves to be cut.

Key
To key a surface is to rub it down or sand it to make it easier for a further surface of paint or varnish to adhere to it.

MDF
Medium density fibreboard, available in various thicknesses.

Masking off
To block out an area that does not require the next layer of paint, with, for example, masking tape.

Mitre box
Using a mitre box in conjunction with a saw enables 45° angle cutting of wood so that the butted pieces make a right angle.

Mosaic tesserae
Small pieces of tile made out of stone, glass or ceramic. They are set into a cement to create a decorative and hard-wearing surface.

Mouldings
Lengths of timber cut with a variety of profiles, to be attached to a surface for decoration.

Nail punch
A tool that allows pins or nails to be hammered just below or flush with the surface of the wood, without the surrounding area of wood becoming knocked or bruised by the head of the hammer.

Open time
The time in which a glaze, size, paint or varnish remains workable before drying.

Paintbrushes
Can refer to heavier decorators' brushes or fine artists' brushes.

Paint scrapers
Metal tools designed to assist the removal of old paint from a surface, either as dry stripping or in conjunction with chemical stripper or a hot-air gun.

Pigment
Finely ground coloured powder that becomes a surface colour or paint

Mosaic tesserae

Mixing dish

Pincers

Decorators' brushes

Sandpaper

Dusting brush

Decorators' comb

Mitre box

when mixed with, for example, oil or water. Pigments are produced from inorganic (mineral) or organic (for example, vegetable, animal) substances.

Pounce pad
For tamping down leaf in gilding. This is a tight pad of a finely woven, lint-free material, ideally silk with cotton wool inside.

Rubbing down
A less harsh method than sanding, using very fine abrasives such as flour paper or fine wire wool.

Sandpaper
Also known as glass paper or abrasive paper, sandpaper is available in grades from very fine for finishing work to coarse grade or grit for heavier work.

Scumble glaze
A medium to which pigment is added to suspend the colour and delay drying time in order to create 'effects'.

Shellac
A resin-based varnish, distilled in alcohol.

To size
In general terms to seal a surface to make it non-porous and able to take the next layer of paint, varnish or decoration evenly and without the risk of it flaking off. In oil gilding to apply a coat of oil size that is rather like a

varnish but with a specific open time.

Softening
A term used of paints, colour and glazes meaning to 'blur' the edges or decoration with the use of, for example, a badger brush, or a soft cloth in a light dabbing motion.

Sponges
Synthetic sponges are good for printing (see cot project on page 26). Natural sponges are best for a paint finish where one colour is sponged over another.

Stretching
Preparation of fabric or canvas on a frame, prior to painting.

Tamping down
Using a soft brush or pounce pad, to press down leaf in gilding to ensure even contact and adhesion to the surface.

Wash
A thinned down layer of, for example, paint; its principal aim is to be relatively transparent and to enhance the colour underneath.

Wiping off
A method of creating a clear line or edge when painting or glazing by wrapping a cloth tightly around the thumb and pulling it along to take excess paint away.

Suppliers

The Bath Knob Shop
2 Hot Street
Bath BA1 1SJ
Tel. 01225 469606
Door furniture and accessories.

H. W. Davies and Son Ltd
Decorators' Merchants
19a Monmouth Place
Bath BA1 2AY
Tel. 01225 425638
Decorating materials.

Great Mills
Head office: Great Mills Retail Ltd
RMC House
Old Mills Trading Estate
Old Mills
Paulton
Bristol BS18 5SX
Tel. 01761 416034
Building and decorating materials.

Hill Leigh (Bath) Ltd
Timber and Builders' Merchants
Sydenham Wharf
Lower Bristol Road
Bath BA2 3EE
Tel. 01225 446110
Timber and fixings.

Homebase Ltd
Head Office: Homebase Ltd
Beddington House
Wallington
Surrey SN6 0HB
Tel. 0181 784 7200
Building and decorating materials.

Romantique Mosaics
12-13 Pulteney Bridge
Bath BA2 4AY
Tel. 01225 463073
Mosaics and mosaic supplies.

Stuart Stevenson
Artists' and Gilders' Suppliers
68 Clerkenwell Road,
London EC1M 5QA
Tel. 0171 253 1693
Paints and gilding materials.

Alec Tiranti Ltd
27 Warren Street
London W1P 5DG
Tel. 0171 636 8565
AND 70 High Street
Theale
Reading
Berks RG7 5AR
Tel. 01189 302775
*Casting, modelling, and sculpting
materials and tools*

Edgar Udney Ltd
314 Balham High Road
London SW17 7AA
Tel. 0181 767 8181
Importers of mosaics and tiles.

Walcot Reclamation Ltd
108 Walcot Street
Bath BA1 5BG
Tel. 01225 444404
*Reclaimed architectural materials,
door knobs, finials, decorative
accessories, architectural antiques.*

Index